Bollywood Dance

I014I002

Marjorie Seevers

xist Publishing

Check out all of the books in the Dancing Through Life Series

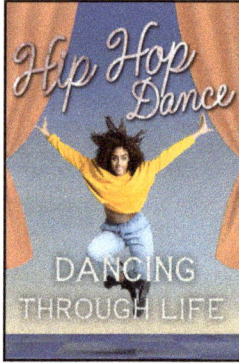

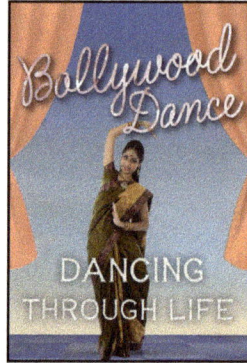

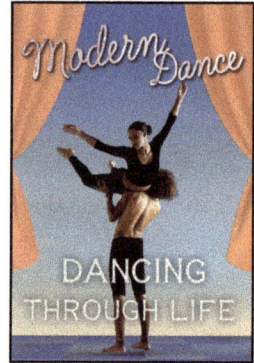

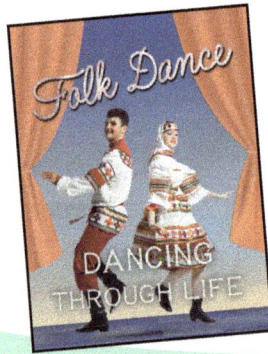

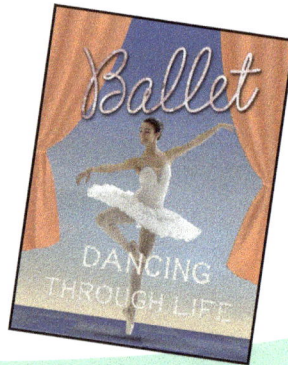

Hip Hop Dance — DANCING THROUGH LIFE

Bollywood Dance — DANCING THROUGH LIFE

Modern Dance — DANCING THROUGH LIFE

Folk Dance — DANCING THROUGH LIFE

Ballet — DANCING THROUGH LIFE

Published in the United States by Xist Publishing
www.xistpublishing.com
© 2025 Copyright Xist Publishing

All images licensed from Adobe Stock

First Edition
Hardcover ISBN: 978-1-5324-5433-2
Paperback ISBN: 978-1-5324-5434-9
eISBN: 978-1-5324-5432-5

PUBLISHED IN TEXAS

Contents

DANCING
THROUGH
LIFE

Chapter 1: What is Bollywood Dance?

Bollywood dance is a fun and lively type of dance that comes from India. It is named after Bollywood, the big movie industry in India, like Hollywood in America. Bollywood dance is a mix of many different dance styles, including classical Indian dance, folk dance, and even modern styles like hip-hop and jazz.

In Bollywood movies, dance is a big part of the story. Dancers use their movements to show feelings like love, happiness, or sadness. The dances are full of energy, bright colors, and big smiles. Bollywood dance is often performed in large groups, with many dancers moving together in rhythm with the music.

One of the special things about Bollywood dance is how it mixes tradition with modern styles. Some Bollywood dances are based on old stories from Indian culture. Others are more modern, with fast moves and trendy music. This mix makes Bollywood dance exciting and fun to watch.

Bollywood dance is more than just steps and moves. It's about expressing joy and telling a story through dance. Whether in a movie or on stage, Bollywood dance always brings a smile to the audience's face.

3

4

History of Bollywood Dance – From Films to the World Stage

Bollywood dance has a rich history. It began in Indian movies. The name "Bollywood" comes from combining "Bombay" and "Hollywood." In the early days, Indian films were silent. But when sound was added, music and dance became important.

The first Bollywood dances were inspired by traditional Indian dance forms. These dances, like Bharatanatyam (BAH-rah-tuh-NAT-yum) and Kathak (KAH-thak), were graceful and told stories. As Bollywood grew, the dances started to include other styles. Folk dances from different parts of India were also used.

In the 1950s and 1960s, Bollywood movies became very popular. Dance numbers became a key part of the films. They helped tell the story and entertain the audience. Famous dancers and choreographers brought new ideas to Bollywood dance. They mixed traditional moves with modern styles. This mix made Bollywood dance exciting and fresh.

As time went on, Bollywood dance started to change. It began to include more styles from around the world. Jazz, hip-hop, and salsa were added. This made the dances lively and fun. The colorful costumes and catchy music made Bollywood movies famous worldwide.

By the 1990s, Bollywood dance had become popular outside of India. Dance groups in many countries began to learn and perform Bollywood dances. Bollywood movies were shown all around the world. People everywhere loved the energy and joy of Bollywood dance.

Bollywood dance continues to evolve. It blends new styles with traditional moves. But the heart of Bollywood dance stays the same. It's all about telling stories, expressing emotions, and having fun.

Chapter 2: Meet the Bollywood Dancer

Who Can Be a Bollywood Dancer?

Anyone can be a Bollywood dancer! Boys and girls of all ages can enjoy Bollywood dance. It doesn't matter where you are from or what your background is. If you love to move to music and express yourself, you can be a Bollywood dancer.

Bollywood dance is for everyone. Some dancers start young, while others begin later in life. You don't need special skills to start. All you need is a passion for dance and a willingness to learn. With practice, anyone can improve and enjoy Bollywood dancing.

Bollywood dancers come in all shapes and sizes. Each dancer brings their own unique style and energy to the dance. Some dancers are more graceful, while others are full of energy. In Bollywood dance, everyone's strengths can shine.

There are many different roles in Bollywood dance. Some dancers perform as part of a group, moving together in sync. Others might take on solo parts, showing off their special skills. Whether in a group or alone, every dancer plays an important role in telling the story.

Bollywood dance is not just for professionals. People dance Bollywood at parties, weddings, and festivals. It's a fun way to celebrate and enjoy music with others. Whether on stage or at home, anyone can join in the fun of Bollywood dance.

So, who can be a Bollywood dancer? The answer is simple: anyone who loves to dance! Whether you dream of being in a movie or just want to have fun, Bollywood dance is for you. All you need is a love for music and the joy of movement.

The Different Roles in Bollywood Dance

In Bollywood dance, there are many roles that dancers can play. Each role helps to tell the story and adds excitement. Whether in a group or solo, each role is important.

One main role in Bollywood dance is the lead dancer. The lead dancer often takes center stage. They perform the most important steps. This dancer may tell the main part of the story through their movements. They capture the audience's attention with their energy.

Another important role is the supporting dancer. Supporting dancers perform alongside the lead dancer. They often dance in groups, moving together on the stage. These dancers add depth to the performance. Even though they are not in the spotlight, their role is crucial.

Chorus dancers are a larger group of dancers. They fill the stage with movement. They often perform in the background, creating the setting. Chorus dancers help make the dance feel big and lively. Their movements may be simpler, but they add to the overall effect.

Sometimes, there are specialty dancers in Bollywood performances. These dancers might perform a unique dance style. They could dance in classical Indian dance or hip-hop. They bring something extra to the performance, adding excitement. There are also character dancers in Bollywood dance. These dancers might play a specific role in the story. They could be a friend, a family member, or even a funny character. They use their movements and expressions to bring their character to life.

Every role in Bollywood dance is important. Each dancer, whether in the front or back, helps tell the story. The different roles work together to create a joyful and colorful dance.

Chapter 3: Bollywood Dance Basics

Basic Steps and Movements

Bollywood dance is known for its fun and lively moves. The basic steps are easy to learn and full of energy. These steps help dancers express joy, excitement, and emotion.

One of the most common steps in Bollywood dance is the hip twist. To do this, dancers move their hips from side to side. The hips often lead the movement, adding a playful and rhythmic feel to the dance.

Another basic movement is the shoulder shimmy. In a shoulder shimmy, dancers quickly shake their shoulders back and forth. This movement adds energy and flair to the dance. It's often used to show excitement or happiness.

The head bob is another common move in Bollywood dance. To do a head bob, dancers move their heads from side to side in time with the music.

Hand gestures are very important in Bollywood dance. Dancers use their hands to tell a story or show emotions. For example, they might place their hands on their hips or raise them above their heads.

The foot tap is a basic step that keeps the rhythm. Dancers tap their feet to the beat of the music. The foot tap is simple but adds energy to the dance. It helps dancers stay in sync with the music and each other.

These basic steps and movements are the foundation of Bollywood dance. They are easy to learn and fun to perform. With practice, dancers can combine these steps to create beautiful and lively dance routines.

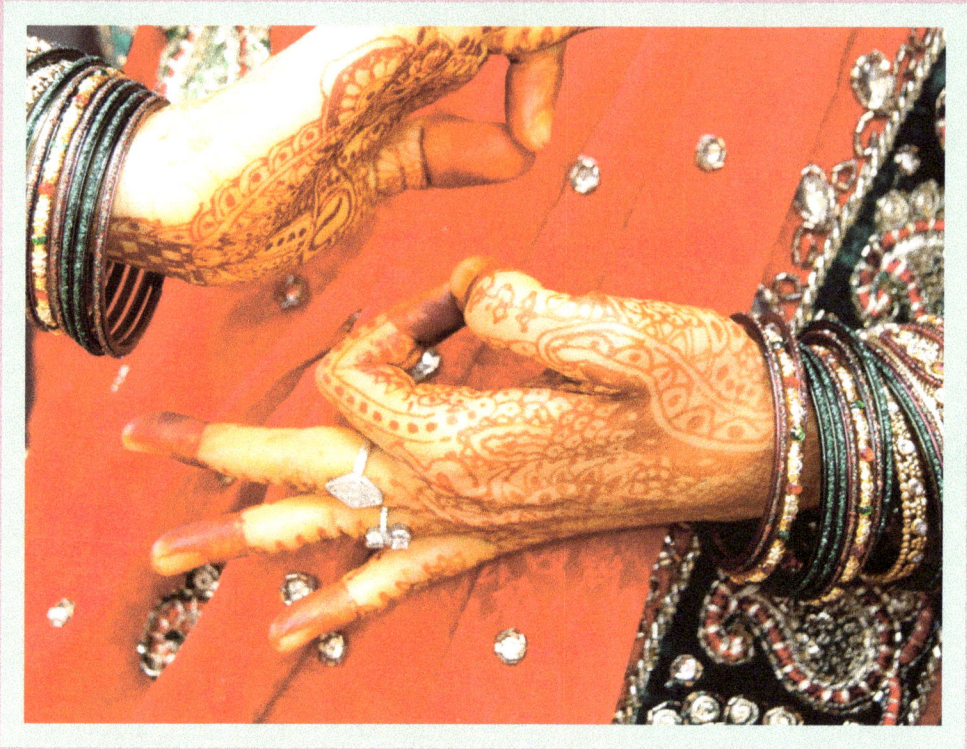

Expressing Emotions Through Dance

One important part of Bollywood dance is facial expressions. Dancers use their faces to show emotions like happiness, sadness, love, or anger. A big smile can show joy, while raised eyebrows might show surprise. These expressions help the audience understand the story.

Hand gestures also play a key role in expressing emotions. Dancers use their hands to add meaning to their movements. For example, hands placed on the heart can show love or affection. Hands raised high can express excitement or celebration. Each gesture adds depth to the dance.

Body movements help to show different feelings. Slow, gentle movements might show calmness or tenderness. Fast, sharp movements can show excitement or anger. The way a dancer moves their body can change the mood of the dance.

Eye movements are another way dancers express emotions. In Bollywood dance, eyes can tell a lot about what a dancer is feeling. Dancers might look up to show hope or down to show sadness. Quick eye movements can show surprise or curiosity. The eyes are very expressive and help to tell the story.

Posture is also important in showing emotions. Standing tall with open arms can show confidence and strength. A slouched posture might show sadness or defeat. The way a dancer holds their body can change how the dance feels.

Bollywood dance is all about connecting with the audience. Dancers use their expressions and movements to bring the story to life. Whether showing joy, love, or sadness, the emotions make the dance more powerful. When dancers express emotions through dance, they make the performance unforgettable.

Chapter 4: Dressing for Bollywood Dance

The Bollywood Outfit: Traditional vs. Modern Styles

Bollywood dance outfits are bright and colorful. The clothes dancers wear make the dance more fun. There are two main styles of Bollywood dance outfits: traditional and modern.

Traditional Bollywood outfits come from Indian culture. Women often wear sarees. A saree is a long piece of fabric wrapped around the body. It is worn with a blouse. The saree is elegant and lets the dancer move easily.

Women might also wear a lehenga. A lehenga is a long skirt with a matching blouse and scarf. Men might wear a kurta, which is a long shirt, with loose pants called pajamas. Traditional outfits are usually made of silk or cotton. They are often decorated with shiny beads or embroidery. These outfits help dancers look graceful and connect with Indian culture.

Modern Bollywood outfits are influenced by today's fashion. They might include leggings, crop tops, or jeans mixed with traditional pieces. For example, a dancer might wear a modern top with a traditional lehenga skirt. This mix of old and new creates a fresh look.

Choosing between traditional and modern styles depends on the dance. Sometimes dancers mix both styles to create a special look. Whether wearing traditional or modern outfits, Bollywood dancers always look bright and ready to perform.

15

Accessories and Makeup in Bollywood Dance

Accessories and makeup are important in Bollywood dance. They add sparkle and style to the dancer's look. Both help make the performance more colorful and fun. Jewelry is a key accessory in Bollywood dance. Dancers often wear bangles on their wrists. The bangles jingle when they move. Earrings, necklaces, and rings are also worn. These pieces are usually bright and shiny. They catch the light and make the dance more beautiful.

Headpieces are another popular accessory. Women might wear a maang tikka, a piece of jewelry that rests on the forehead. It's often decorated with gems or pearls. Headpieces make the dancer look elegant and royal.

Scarves and dupattas are also used in Bollywood dance. A dupatta is a long scarf worn over the shoulders or around the head. It adds grace to the dancer's movements. Scarves can be twirled or tossed during the dance to create pretty patterns in the air.

Makeup is just as important as accessories. It helps to show the dancer's facial expressions. Dancers wear bright lipstick and blush to make their faces stand out. They also use eyeliner and eyeshadow to make their eyes look bigger. Bold makeup helps the audience see the dancer's emotions.

Henna designs are sometimes used as well. Henna is a natural dye used to draw patterns on the hands and feet. These designs are beautiful and connect the dancer to Indian traditions.

In Bollywood dance, accessories and makeup are more than just decorations. They help to tell the story and bring the dance to life. Each piece adds to the overall look, making the performance shine. With the right accessories and makeup, a dancer feels confident and ready to perform.

Chapter 5: The Big Performance

Preparing for the Stage

Getting ready for a big performance takes a lot of work. Dancers must be ready both in body and mind. Preparing for the stage starts long before the show begins.

First, dancers practice their routines many times. They learn every step and movement until they can do them perfectly. This practice builds confidence and helps the dancers feel ready.

Next, dancers prepare their costumes and accessories. Each costume must fit perfectly. They also check their accessories, like jewelry and headpieces, to ensure everything is in place. Dancers also prepare their shoes, making sure they are comfortable and secure.

On the day of the performance, dancers arrive at the theater early. They need time to warm up their muscles. Dancers stretch and do exercises to get their bodies ready for the performance.

After warming up, dancers put on their costumes and makeup. Makeup helps to make their faces look bright and expressive under the stage lights. Hair is styled neatly, often in a bun, to keep it out of the way during the dance.

When everything is ready, the dancers wait backstage. They listen for their cue to go on stage. Each dancer feels a mix of excitement and nerves. But they are ready to give their best performance.

Preparing for the stage is a big part of being a dancer. It takes hard work and dedication. But all the effort is worth it when the dancers step into the spotlight and bring their performance to life.

The Joy of Performing Bollywood Dance

Performing Bollywood dance on stage is a special experience. After all the hard work and practice, it's time to shine. The joy of performing comes from sharing the dance with the audience.

When the music starts, dancers feel the excitement. They move with energy and grace, telling the story through their dance. Each step, hand movement, and expression is done with care. The dancers feel proud of what they have learned and practiced.

As they dance, the audience watches closely. The bright lights and colorful costumes make the stage feel magical. Dancers connect with the music and with the people watching. They express emotions like happiness, love, and excitement through their movements. The joy of dancing comes from this connection.

Hearing applause from the audience makes the dancers feel appreciated. Each clap shows that the audience enjoyed the performance. This makes the dancers feel happy and proud. It shows that all their hard work has paid off.

Performing in a group adds to the joy. Bollywood dance is often done with many dancers moving together. Dancers support each other on stage, creating a sense of teamwork. They move in sync, making the performance beautiful and lively.

The joy of performing Bollywood dance stays with the dancers even after the show ends. They feel a sense of accomplishment. They know they have done their best and shared something special. This feeling inspires them to keep dancing and improving.

Conclusion

Bollywood dance is a way to express joy and tell stories. It helps connect people through movement and music. From learning steps to performing, Bollywood dance teaches practice, teamwork, and creativity.

Bollywood dance is full of color, energy, and emotion. Whether you are new to dancing or have danced for years, there is always something fun to learn. Bollywood dance is for everyone, no matter your age or background. It's about enjoying yourself and sharing your love of dance.

Anyone can be a Bollywood dancer. You just need to try. Whether you dream of performing on stage or dancing for fun, Bollywood dance is for you. Keep dancing, keep smiling, and let Bollywood inspire you.

Your journey with Bollywood dance is just starting. There is so much more to explore. Whether you dance alone or in a group, Bollywood dance will bring joy and energy into your life. Keep the music playing, and let your love for dance shine.

Glossary

Bollywood   A nickname for the Hindi-language film industry based in Mumbai, India.

Bharatanatyam   A traditional Indian classical dance form with intricate footwork.

Choreographer   A person who creates and arranges dance movements for performances.

Dupatta   A long scarf worn by Indian women, often part of dance costumes.

Expressive   Dance A dance style using movements and facial expressions to tell a story.

Folk Dance   Traditional dances from various regions of India, influencing Bollywood.

Hip Twist   A Bollywood dance move where the hips are moved side to side.

Kathak   A classical North Indian dance known for storytelling through movement.

Lehenga   A traditional long skirt paired with a blouse and scarf.

Maang Tikka   Traditional Indian forehead jewelry often worn in dance performances.

Saree   A long fabric draped around the body, often worn in Bollywood dances.

Index

www.ingramcontent.com/pod-product-compliance
Lightning Source LLC
LaVergne TN
LVHW070834080426

835508LV00027B/3446